LONDON DOCKLANDS

Professor S K Al Naib

The Port of London, August 1964, was the greatest port in the world.

Fourth Edition March 1994

D0316583

ISBN 0-901987-81-6

BUSY SCENE IN THE ROYAL DOCKS

Visitors to London Docklands watch with intense interest the great activity among vessels in King George V Dock on 12 August 1932. The paddle steamer launch was pulled by means of a Port of London Authority tug. The excursion started from Tower Pier through the Pool, Limehouse, Greenwich, Blackwall, Woolwich and Gallions and the Royal Docks.

On a beautiful summer day, the people are dressed in light clothing of that particular period but many are wearing hats! The trippers are also enjoying their picnic lunch!

On the north side of the Dock, left of picture, the ship in the foreground is the American SS Abraham Lincoln, loading bagged cargo from a barge, possibly sugar bags from the nearby Tate & Lyle refinery. The adjacent vessel is a British India ship loading export cargo for the Indian sub-continent. Note the goose-neck type of quayside cranes made by Babcock & Wilcock. On the south side, the two ships are discharging and loading Australian and New Zealand cargoes. The quayside cranes were made by Stothart & Pitt.

At the centre of the picture, an old London sailing barge is proceeding towards the lock entrance followed by a loaded barge with a lighterman manually rowing the barge!

The Royal Docks were closed around 1980 and in 1987 the new London City Airport runway was built on the north side of the Dock (see page 34). For complete information on present day Docklands please see the book "Discover London Docklands" published and reprinted in 1992 and 1993.

ISBN 0-901 987-81-6
First Printing March 1990
Second Printing May 1991
Third Printing March 1993
The first and second printings of 5000 copies of this book were sold out recently and it is now reprinted to meet continuing demand. Special thanks are due to the public for their kind support.

Books by the author
"Dockland" Historical Survey
"London Docklands" Past, Present and Future
"European Docklands", Past, Present and Future
(Companion to London Docklands)
"Hydraulic Structures" Theory, Analysis and Design
"Discover London Docklands" A to Z Illustrated Guide
"Applied Hydraulics" Theory and Worked Examples
"21st Century London" Guide to Greatest Attractions
(Forthcoming)

The author is Head of Department of Civil Engineering at the University of East London, England.

Printed by Ashmead Press, London.

Preface

A major new book on historic docklands provides a vivid portrait of development from the eighteenth century to the present day. It contains over 130 illustrations, many of which provide a lasting memory for those who love these old places with their enchanting warehouses and vast water areas.

Today's docklands are undergoing enormous changes. Their heritage, being a vital part of our history, provides a foundation on which the future of these areas can safely be built.

London Docklands are now recognized as the largest and most successful urban regeneration in the world and the biggest that has been undertaken in London since the Great Fire of 1666. Utilising the redundant dock water areas as unique environmental features, new commercial and residential projects are emerging along the old docks of St Katharine, Wapping and Isle of Dogs.

Similar transformations have taken place in most European ports. The old docklands, often located close to the city centre, are no longer used for port activities and offer a major opportunity for regeneration and economic revival.

The main aims of the book are:

1   To update the historical 'Dockland' book by the editor in 1986 and to bring the story of London Docklands up to 1989 and into the future.

2   To review and compare developments in London Docklands with a number of port areas in Europe in view of the impending significance of 1992 and the EEC open Common Market opportunities. A companion book on European Docklands is being published separately to enable this to be done.

In the United Kingdom and many parts of the world there are commitments to regenerating the old docklands. London Docklands is considered as an outstanding success in this respect. It has problems typical of those encountered elsewhere and the solutions that can be offered. In fact it can act as a model for the future. Britain is now the world leader in this field.

The book provides an authoritative and unique reference for the general public, local authorities, private and commercial developers, Government departments and other organisations. It is suitable for use in schools and colleges for the study of the history and development of London docklands and the way in which their future will reflect the past of these historically important areas.

An invitation to the reader.

If you are a reader with experience of or unpublished information on docklands in any part of the world, or with interesting stories of life and work in London Docklands, or can assist in any Docklands research, please contact:

Dr S K Al Naib
Head of Department of Civil Engineering
Polytechnic of East London
Longbridge Road, Dagenham
Essex, RM8 2AS
England

Telephone: 081-590 7722

Contents

Great Britain

London Docklands

Dr S K Al Naib

Early History

The Port of London has been a major international port since its establishment by the Romans in 50 AD and became of vital importance in the history of the UK and the British Empire. Not a great deal is known about the size or form of the port before the sixteenth century but around 1560, at the outset of Queen Elizabeth's reign, a Royal Commission was set up to select and appoint licensed wharves where all goods entering the port should be landed. Twenty 'Legal Quays' were established along the north bank of the river between London Bridge and Tower Bridge, under the surveillance of Custom Officers who daily attended them.

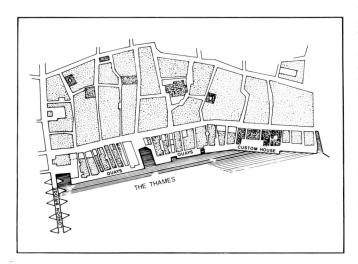

1   Map of the Legal Quays established around 1560 along the north bank of the River Thames between London Bridge and Tower Bridge where all dutiable goods entered the country up to 1796. (PLA)

The period from 1500 to 1800 witnessed the growth of world wide English trade and established London as its financial centre. Although this trade was created and controlled by the merchants of London, it was served by the inhabitants of the riverside areas east of the city known as London Dockland. The building and manning of an increasing number of ships stimulated the growth and transformation of the Dockland area, particularly between London Bridge and Blackwall. It was here that the demands of the industrial and commercial revolution transformed sparsely populated rural areas into a densely packed urban and industrial Port of London.

This rapid expansion caused serious problems of congestion in the Port in the second half of the eighteenth century. By 1790, trade in the port had tripled, while the average tonnage of ships had doubled from 50 tonnes to 100 tonnes over the previous 100 years. Although there was room at the mooring piers for 600 ships there were occasions when seasonal traders, such as those carrying sugar from the West Indies, swelled the numbers in port to as many as 1400 ships. The inadequacy of the existing quays in handling the growing quantities of merchandise meant that ships often moored in the river for months blocking the passage of other vessels and providing a source of plunder for pilferers and river pirates.

It became evident that unless wharfage for ships was increased, the future development of London as a trading centre of the world would suffer. After a period of petitioning by merchants and debate by Parliament (1793-99) plans for building the first commercial wet docks for cargo handling were approved. The decision to allow other than the legal quays to handle dutiable goods marked the beginning of a new period in the life of the Port and the start of a major programme of dock construction.

Nineteenth Century Era

The West India Dock Act of 1799 and London Dock Act of 1800 enabled the construction of two docks. The Engineer for the West India Dock was William Jessop who designed a 12ha import dock and 9.6ha export dock on the Isle of Dogs for the West India Dock Company. The import dock opened in 1802 and the export dock in 1806. The London Dock was built concurrently on an 8ha site near Wapping with John Rennie, the elder, as the Engineer for the London Dock Company. This dock was opened in 1805 at the same time as the City Canal across the Isle of Dogs to the south of the West India Docks.

Both the above companies were highly profitable paying shareholders a maximum 10% dividend between 1803 and 1829 and their success led to further building. The East India Docks with a water area of 26ha were opened in 1806 with John Rennie and James Walker as the Engineers. To the south of the river, the Grand Surrey Canal Company opened its own dock in 1807.

When the 21 year monopolies of the above dock companies expired, Thomas Telford, as Designer/Engineer, and Philip Hardwick, as Architect were commissioned to construct the elegant St. Katharine Docks which were opened in 1828 at an expensive site between London Dock and the Tower. Practically all the buildings are now demolished but the docks themselves are a tourist attraction, the basins being used as a yacht marina which includes the National Maritime Trust's collection of historic ships.

All the aforementioned "Georgian" Docks were designed for wooden sailing ships which, for structural reasons, seldom exceeded 1,000 tonnes gross. The advent of iron steamships with 5,000 to 8,000 tonnes gross and sometimes bigger, meant that larger docks were required. This started the second phase of building - the "Victorian" Docks.

2 *Custom Houses in the Port of London. (a) The Old Custom House of the Legal Quays seen from the river, with the Tower of London to the east, based on an engraving by J Bowler 1753. (b) The busy port and the New Custom House about a hundred years later 1842. (PLA)*

The Royal Victoria Dock opened in 1855 with George Parker Bidder the Engineer and Designer, and Peto, Brassey & Betts, the contractors. The promoters were men from the new world of railways rather than those with traditional shipping interests. It was the first dock to be built specifically for steamships and also the first to incorporate hydraulic machinery for the purpose of opening and closing the lock gates. The dock and tidal basin were designed to enclose 34.6ha surrounded by 1.6 km of quay and wharfage. The Victoria Dock was extended in 1880 by the addition of the Royal Albert Dock and all were operated by the London and St Katharine Dock Company founded in 1864.

With the opening of the Royal Docks and in particular the prestigious Albert Dock, the East and West India Dock Company faced fierce competition and lost considerable trade. To avert losses, the Company built, in 1886, a new deep water dock of 30ha at Tilbury, 25 km downstream from the Royals and 40 km from the centre of London.

Twentieth Century Era

In 1889 The Dock Companies combined to form the London and India Docks Joint Committee. Shipping was continually getting larger and to allow its passage up the Thames the river had to be dredged and deepened. The private companies were unable to afford this improvement and were subsequently nationalised by the Government who established the Port of London Authority (PLA) in 1909. The PLA took responsibility for operating and maintaining all docks and undertook to deepen the river from the estuary to the Royal Docks. A channel not less than 9m deep at low water was constructed at a cost of £2.5m while another £4.5m was spent on improvements and extensions.

The thriving conditions which prevailed in the docks immediately after the First World War prompted the PLA to extend the Albert Dock by the construction of the George V Dock, designed by Mr. Frederick Palmer, their first Chief Engineer. The dock contained a water area of nearly 26ha and a dry dock 229m long by 30.5m wide. Work started in 1912 but was delayed by the early years of the war. It was eventually opened by King George V on 8 July 1921; at a cost of approximately £4.0m.

This was virtually the end of major dock building in the area, but a number of warehouses and jetties were constructed later which included some of the earliest examples of reinforced and prestressed concrete construction dating back to the original licenced Hennebique System.

After the heavy bomb damage of the Second World War, there were major efforts of reconstruction in the dockland. By the early 1960s trade reached a new peak. Over 100 ships a day were using the Royal Docks and the port as a whole was handling over 65 million tonnes of cargo a year.

The PLA invested further in mechanizing cargo handling, new storage sheds and a major £1.3m reconstruction of the Royal Victoria Dock western entrance by the contractors, John Mowlem.

Within a period of two years, there was a revolution in shipping technology and cargo handling. These techniques included containerisation and roll-on roll-off terminals which meant that large numbers of dockers were no longer necessary. Of the 30,000 dockers once employed by the PLA only 3,000 are now needed to cope with about 50 million tonnes of goods a year concentrated at Tilbury Docks.

Ships were no longer willing to take a day coming up river to London and the old docks started to close. The East India Docks closed in 1967, St. Katharine's in 1968, and the London and Surrey Docks in 1969. Despite some attempt to retain a group of docks up river, the West India and Millwall docks closed in 1970 and the Royal Docks in 1985.

Debates on the future of the Port and Docklands have been going on since the late 1960s. Numerous study reports have been produced for the redevelopment of the area, which have been the basis of public consultation. Long term forecasting for the port is difficult, as it is affected by the pattern of

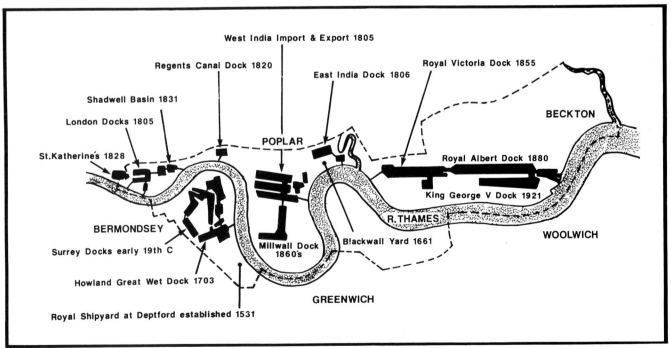

3   The sequence of dock development in the Port of London during the nineteenth century which was to revolutionize the position of London as a trading centre of the world.

international trade and by the degree of competition between British ports. The old Docklands, however, offer a major opportunity for regeneration and improvement of life in East London.

This book begins by outlining the historical background and construction in the Port of London, draws together some of the surviving engineering and architectural features and finally attempts to provide a summary of current development and future rebuilding.

4   *The Port of London seen from a balloon c 1902. A birds' eye view of the docks was made by Mr Charles Williams from sketches taken at a height of over 2,000 ft (610 m) above the River Thames during a balloon trip. (ILN)*

Construction in Port of London

The nineteenth century was an exciting period of dock construction which was to revolutionise the position of London as a trading centre of the world. The initiative for expansion came from the merchants of London and in particular William Vaughan, a London insurance director and Fellow of the Royal Society. In 1793, the year of the outbreak of the war with France, Vaughan published a treatise on Wet Docks, Quays and Warehouses for the Port of London, with hints respecting Trade. He advocated that a major improvement of the port depended upon the building of enclosed tide-free docks with warehouses under the control of customs officers. He identified St. Katharine's in Wapping, Isle of Dogs and Rotherhithe, as suitable sites along the river.

Following this lead, city merchants, ship owners and private investors commissioned many famous engineers and architects of the period including Daniel Alexander, Ralph Walker, William Jessop, John Rennie, Thomas Telford and George Parker Bidder. They planned and built a magnificent series of linked docks with locks and warehouses which enabled the ships of the British Empire and the world to trade more efficiently and to create the economic miracle of the industrial revolution. The construction work naturally features in every aspect of the history of the old Docklands and their future development. An attempt is made in this section to bring the descriptions of the various construction projects together and to indicate what impacts they may have on the future character of the area in which detailed designs make the river once again a focus of great construction and commercial activity.

Nearly 200 years ago, the dock areas were largely undeveloped marsh land and were subjected to frequent flooding by the river Thames. They were covered by recent alluvium deposits overlying flood plain gravels which in turn overlaid London clay, sand beds and chalk. In the course of the construction of the docks, the sites in the immediate vicinity were raised by the placing of up to 4 meter fills obtained from the dock excavations. Because of the compressible nature of the fill and of the alluvium deposits, the majority of dock buildings had to be supported on piers or driven piles founded within the gravel.

In designing the docks and their structures, civil engineers had to take into consideration not only the ground conditions and the peculiarities of the sites, but also the nature and volume of the traffic to be accommodated, financial restraints and other circumstances which largely governed the design of the docks and their ultimate cost effectiveness. In this respect the West India Docks were a remarkable example of a successful engineering and commercial project in the history of the Port of London.

West India Docks

The West India Docks complex, completed by 1806, consisted of the Import and Export Docks, the entrance basins of Blackwall and Limehouse and the City Canal. The Import Dock was 800m long by 155m wide and 7m deep. The quays were 2m above Trinity High Water Level so the walls rose to a height of 9m above dock bottom. They had a curved vertical section and were constructed in brickwork approximately 2m thick at the top, with counterforts bonded into the wall by iron reinforcement and coping stones. The walls were backed with puddle clay and a layer of clay blanketed the dock bottom to reduce the loss of water by seepage through the gravel stratum. The Blackwall Basin had an entrance lock 59m long by 15m wide and a depth of over 7m. The lock gates, built in oak, and slightly curved in plan, were supported on rollers running on iron sweeps and operated by capstan and chains. The Limehouse Basin was 47m long by 11m wide and just under 7m deep with a double-leaf swing bridge crossing the lock.

Nine warehouses, five storeys high plus a basement and attic, were built along the north quay. They had external brick walls with timber columns and beams supporting wooden floors. Internal brick walls, with iron doors, divided each warehouse into three sections for fire proofing purposes. These warehouses were used mainly for the storage of sugar, coffee and casks of rum in the basements.

The Export Dock was 800m long by 120m wide with a depth of 7m. No warehouses were required as cargoes went directly into the outward bound ships from lighters. The locks leading from the two basins into the dock had practically the same dimensions as those into the Import Dock, and the western lock could be crossed by a swing bridge.

The East and West India Dock Company decided in 1866 to increase their system of docks by enlarging and reconstructing the South Dock, formerly known as the City Canal. The South Dock was designed by the engineer, Mr. J C Hawkshaw, and built by the contractor, George Wythes. It was opened in March 1870.

The main dock was 815m long by 138m wide and had quay walls all round it. On the north side of the dock there were 16 jetties affording accommodation for 33 vessels and opposite each jetty down the centre of the dock were buoys for mooring the vessels. The west entrance to the City Canal was retained, while a new entrance was constructed at the eastern end leading from the river to the basin. The curved gates were of

5   The splendid West India Docks on the Isle of Dogs were the first wet docks built for cargo handling with extensive, well policed, warehousing. (a) An elevated view westward of the docks and warehouses on the eve of completion 1806 from an engraving by William Daniell. (PLA). (b) An aerial photograph of the docks after their closure 1970. (LDDC)

6   *The superb London Docks were built in Wapping 1805. (a) A view of the docks from the west 1808, from an aquatint by William Daniell. (PLA) (b) An aerial photograph of the same docks on 30 August 1968 just before their closure. (Handford Photography)*

7   The opening of St Katharine Docks, and warehouses took place on 25 October 1828. This painting by W J Huggins marks the occasion with the first ship entering the dock. (PLA)

8   The lively Port of London in the middle of the nineteenth century. Activities in the port looking westward below London Bridge August 1862. (PLA)

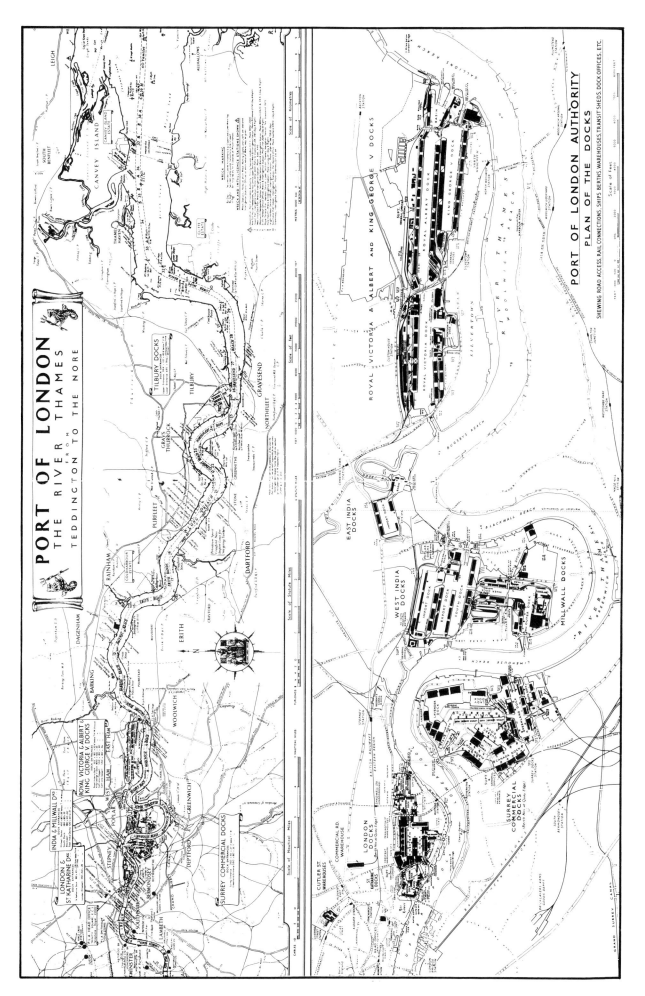

9   Port of London Authority around 1955. General map of the docks along the River Thames with extensive concentration of docks, warehouses, and transit sheds which could not be rivalled anywhere else in the world. (PLA)

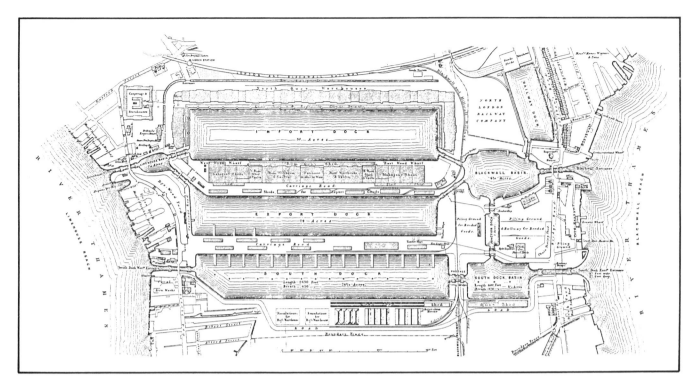

10 Map of the West India Docks 1870 following the enlargement and reconstruction of the South Dock, formerly known as the City Canal. The South Dock was designed by the Engineer, J.C Hawkshaw and built by the contractor, George Wythes. (ICE)

iron with timber posts and sills. They were cellular in construction with two skins formed of iron plates separated by and riveted to the horizontal and vertical ribs.

12 The Old Gateway to the West India Import Dock, opened for business in September 1802. (LDDC)

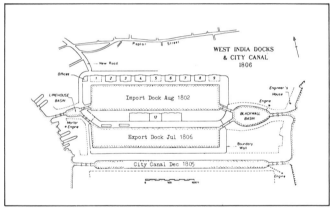

11 Map of the West India Docks and City Canal opened 1802-6 for trade with the West Indies. The Engineer for the West India Dock Company was William Jessop who designed the Import and Export Docks. (PLA)

East India Docks

The East India Docks were built on a site at Blackwall and incorporated the Brunswick Dock completed earlier in 1790. Like the West India Docks, they consisted of a basin communicating with an Import and Export Dock. The entrance lock was 64m long by 14m wide with a sill depth of over 7m below Trinity High Water. The Export Dock area was sold by the PLA and since 1951 the site has been occupied by the Brunswick Electricity Company.

Millwall Dock

In 1865 the Millwall Freehold Land and Dock Company started work on the construction of the Millwall Dock, on a 81 ha site to the south of the West India Docks. John Fowler was the designer and John Aird the contractor.

The dock, completed in 1868, was reversed L-shaped with a 24m wide entrance lock into the river at Limehouse Reach. It had a water area of 15 ha and quays each side extending up to the boundary of the South Dock with which it was connected by a channel.

The dock had the first granary built in the Port of London for the Baltic grain market and the first dry dock in an impounded dock for maintenance and repair of ships. The sheds along the quayside were mainly two storeys high with low headroom of 2.75m to take two layers of hogsheads. The dock entrance was damaged during the Second World War and was not reopened.

London and St Katharine Docks

The Western Dock of the London Docks and the Wapping Basin were the original works excavated following the approval of the London merchants' plan by Parliament in 1800. The dock was opened in 1805 to which were added the Eastern Dock (1828), Shadwell Old Basin (1831) and Shadwell New Basin (1858).

The western dock consisted of a rectangular dock, 385m long by 210m wide and 7.6m deep, a communicating lock of 49m between gates and a basin of 1.2 ha. The entrance lock 55m long by 13.7m wide and 7.6m deep, could only accommodate the sailing ships of the time. In later years the dock was served by lighters ferrying goods from the lower locks.

The warehouses of the London Dock became bonded warehouses for imports of rice, tobacco, wine, brandy and genera. Extensive vaults under all the warehouses and quays of the Western Dock stored wines and spirits, with the heavy wines (port and sherry) to be found in the Crescent Vaults. The brick vaulting, about 2.5m in height, below the warehouses and transit sheds was supported by a forest of stone pillars, the whole labyrinth being ventilated by a system of tunnels which helped to maintain an approximate temperature of 60 F so important for the maturing of the wines and spirits stored there.

In 1824, plans were prepared for the construction of St Katharine Docks. These consisted of an entrance lock with three pairs of gates to maintain the water level. On three sides of the docks, there were high warehouses having their front walls supported on massive iron columns on the edge of the quay. By 1830 the total expenditure on construction, including the heavy cost of purchasing and clearing existing property on the site, was of the order of £2m.

In 1836 the St Katharine Dock Company purchased the massive Cutler Street Warehouses from the East India Dock Company. These treasure warehouses, built in 1782 between Middlesex Street and Houndsditch, were five storeys high and covered over 6 ha with 60,000 square metres of floor area. Enclosed stone staircases were provided to allow access to each of the bonded areas. They were specially designed to house and safeguard such valuable cargoes as indigo, opium, marble, tortoise-shell and scent.

In the 1920s, after the collapse of the Turkish Empire, Cutler Street became the market place for carpet distribution where fine carpets from all over the world were held for re-export.

13   The West India Import Dock. The warehouses on the North Quay were used for the storage of molasses, coffee and cotton. The South Quay had mahogany sheds and vaults for storing rum. (a) A view of the dock published in 1818 from an engraving by L C Varall for the Walks through London. (b) Vessels and lighters (boats) for unloading in the dock c1900. (PLA)

14   A bustling scene at the West India Docks seen from the south east 1830, from a lithograph by William Parrott. (PLA)

Tea from India and Ceylon were also held there. In the basement a bottling department existed with as many as 10,000 bottles of wine being distributed from the warehouse daily.

Both the above systems of docks were sited in a built-up area with other properties adjacent to the dock wall, and consequently expansion was restricted in the area. Vertical expansion was also very difficult because of the danger of overloading old quays, almost all of which were honeycombed by vaults. Site restrictions were at their worst in St. Katharine Docks with its long length of quay.

15   An impressive view of the East India Docks opened 1806 to the design of the Engineers John Rennie and Ralph Walker, from an aquatint by William Daniell. (PLA)

16   The important tea trade at the East India Docks. (a) Unloading tea ships at the docks c 1867. (b) Tea clippers and lighters in the docks c 1892. (HPL)

17   Millwall Dock on the Isle of Dogs. (a) The opening of the dock on 13 March 1868. (b) The dock had the first granary built for the Baltic trade in the Port of London c 1900. (PLA)

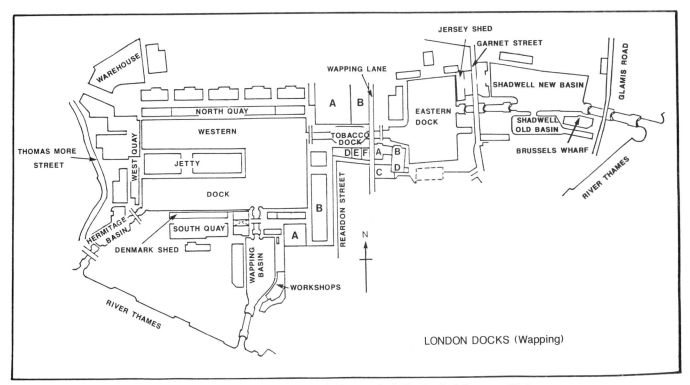

18   *Map of the London Docks from 1805 with John Rennie, the elder, as the Engineer for the London Dock Company. (PLA)*

19   *An elevated view of the River Thames and the magnificent London Docks at Wapping 1803. The picture, based on an engraving by William Danniell, shows hundreds of ships moored in the port. These suffered from extensive pilferage and river piracy prior to the establishment of the River Police Force, in 1798, the first in the world. (PLA)*

20   *The London Docks at Wapping. (a) The shipping entrance from an engraving by J C Varral for the Walks through London published 1817. (b) Shipping wild animals in the docks May 1864. (HPL)*

22   The thriving wine trade at London Docks. Extensive vaults under the warehouses of the Western Basin stored wines and spirits, with port and sherry to be found in the Crescent Vaults. (a) A group photograph of administrative and cooperage staff during their lunch break! (b) Wine testing at the entrance to the Vaults 1896. (GLRO)

21   London Docks at the close of the nineteenth century (a) The bonded warehouses and sheds along the North Quay and shipping in the Western Docks about 1896. (b) Unloading cargoes along the Quay. (GLRO)

23   The London Docks at night by Gustor Dore' 1870. (HPL)

24   Breaking bulk on board a tea ship in the London Docks. December 1877. (HPL)

14

25(a) A view of the elegant St Katharine Docks l845. They were designed by the Engineer Thomas Telford and the Architect Philip Hardwick and built on a restricted site east of the Tower of London. (ILN) (b) An aerial view of the redeveloped St Katharine Docks 1988. (Handford)

26   St Katharine Docks. (a) An elevation of the B warehouse from the Central Island September 1967. (b) A view of the other side of the same warehouses looking east from St Katharine's Way, 1973. (GLRO). (c) A view of the World Trade Centre built on the site of the B Warehouses 1987. (St Katharine by the Tower)

27   The Cutler Street Warehouses, E1. These treasure warehouses, built in 1782 between Middlesex Street and Houndsditch, were specially designed to house and safeguard such valuable cargoes as indigo, opium, marble, tortoise-shell and scent. (a) The main entrance building in the old days. (b) The hand operated hoist machinery on the fifth floor of the S block, 1971. (GLRO)

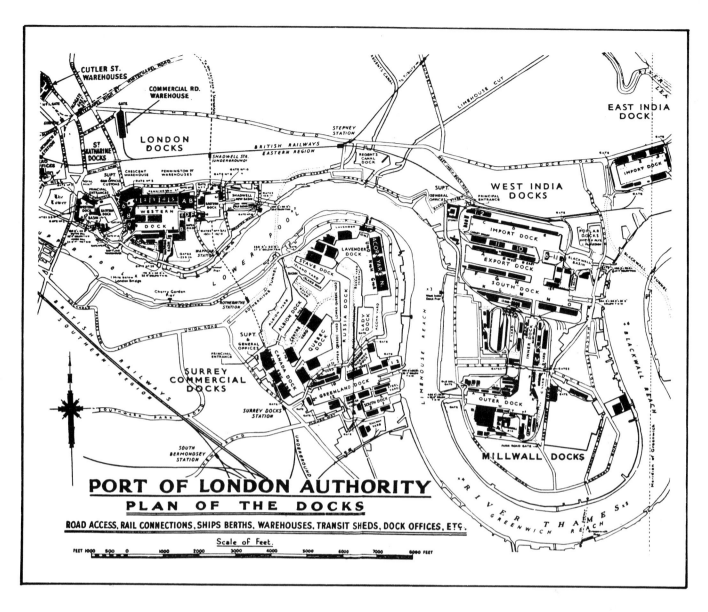

28   *London Docklands in the 1950s. General map of the West India, Surrey Commercial, London and St Katharine Docks along the River Thames with extensive concentration of docks, warehouses and sheds. (PLA)*

The Royal Docks

The Royal Docks consisted of the Royal Victoria Dock opened in 1855, the Royal Albert Dock opened in 1880 and the King George V Dock opened in 1921, each new dock connecting with the older and forming an enclosed water area of 100ha and a dock estate of 446ha. The Victoria Dock entrance was 14km below London Bridge and about 38km above Gravesend, where vessels had to stop for HM Customs, the Port Medical Officer and to change pilots.

The Victoria Dock consisted of a main dock and a tidal basin, all excavated in marsh land. On the north side four solid piers were built, each 152m long by 43m wide and containing a two-storey brick warehouse with vaults. Later, several intermediate timber jetties and considerable accommodation in the way of sheds, warehouses, granaries and refrigerating chambers were added to approximately 49,000 square metres of fireproof warehouses.

The length of quays available for berths was 3,600m and in addition, 900m was leased to various firms for flour mills, coal wharves, etc. The dock was the first dock to be connected into the national railway grid through the North Woolwich branch of the Great Eastern Railway. It was also the first dock to be built for steamships and was the first to incorporate hydraulic power for the operation of the lock gates, etc. The lock was 100m long by 25m wide with a depth of 8.5m below Trinity High Water (THW). The depth of the dock and the inner sill of the lock was 7.8m below THW. As the depth of water over the sill at neap tides was 7.3m any vessel requiring more draught had to wait for spring tides. These conditions prevailed until the opening of the Royal Albert Dock when steam pumps were installed at the end of the new dock to maintain the water of both docks at the level of THW.

The Royal Albert Dock consisted of a main dock 2,200m long with a width of 122m and a depth of 8.3m. The Manor Way passage 24.5m wide by 8.3m deep and a basin of 5.7 ha lead to a lock 168m long by 24.5m wide and 9.1m deep. Here the walls

17

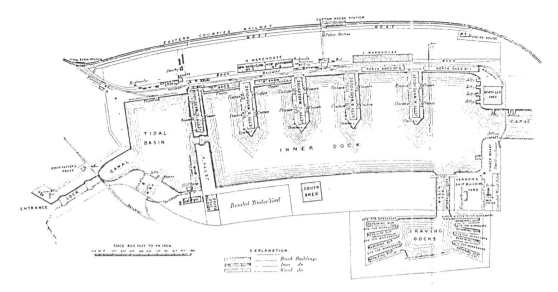

29 *Map of the Royal Victoria Dock and Graving Docks opened 1855. George Parker Bidder was the Engineer/Entrepreneur and Peto, Brassey and Betts the Contractors. It was the first dock to be built for steamships and the first to incorporate hydraulic machinery for the purpose of opening and closing the lock gates and operating the lift to the graving lock. (ICE)*

30 *The Royal Victoria Dock during construction on Plaistow Marshes September 1854. The illustration shows the building of the abutment walls and piling work for the Western Entrance Lock. (ILN)*

31 *A view of the Royal Victoria Dock February 1856 showing the Western Lock at Busby Reach with the old swing bridge and tramway. (ILN)*

32   The Royal Albert Dock at North Woolwich on the eve of completion in June l880. (a) The steel gates of the entrance lock. (b) Manor Way Passage, showing the swing bridge. (c) General view of the dock looking eastward. (ILN)

33   Past scenes of the Royal Docks. (a) Hydraulic lifts were used to float ships at the Victoria Græving Dock December l858. (ILN) (b) Unloading the Arawa and other ships at the Albert Dock l870. (HPL) (c) Busy shipping and lighterage at King George V Dock l930. (LDDC).

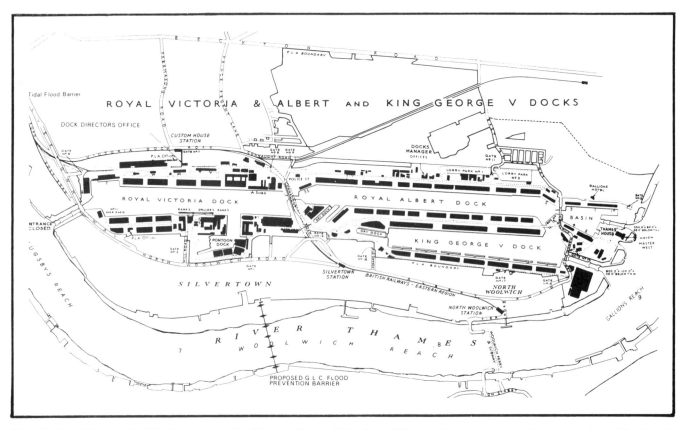

34   *The Royal Docks in the 1950s. General map of the Victoria, Albert and King George V Docks with their extensive modern facilities for world wide trade.* (PLA)

35   *Custom Buildings in the Royal Docks 1977. (a) The Custom House of the Royal Victoria Dock built 1855. (b) The Entrance Building at the Albert Dock dating to 1880.* (GLRO)

were built of concrete faced with gault bricks to minimize the abrasion along the sides of ships. The limited depth led to the construction of the lower lock in 1886 with a depth of 11m. The dock was provided with two dry docks and had a quay 4,622m long available for berths.

On average 1,800 navvies, 48 horses, 14 locomotives, 600 railway wagons, 3 steam engines and about 20 km of temporary railways were used for the massive excavation work. Approximately 3.6 million cubic metres of soil were excavated and placed in the surrounding areas.

In 1912 the Port of London Authority commenced work on the improvement of the Royal Docks by the construction of the King George V Dock, south of the Albert Dock. The dock comprised a wet dock, 26ha in extent, having a depth of 11.6m of water and a total quay length of just over 3.2 km, giving berthing accommodation for 14 large vessels. The entrance lock from the river was 244m long by 30.5m wide with a depth of water over the sill of 13.7m. The dry dock was 229m long and 30.5m wide with a depth of 10.7m of water over the keel blocks. The wet dock was connected to the Royal Albert Dock by a passage 30.5m wide with a depth of 10.4m.

A feature of the wet dock was the provision of reinforced concrete jetties parallel to the south quay wall, with a barge passage between the jetties and the quay. Cranes on the jetties worked the ships' cargo either into barges or to the quay and transit sheds as required. Three sets of interchangeable gates were built into the entrance dock.

36   *An aerial photograph of the Royal Victoria, Albert and King George V Docks at the height of their operations 1960. The spectacular view looking westward shows the concentration of ships along a total quay of over 20 km. (Handford)*

Surrey Commercial Docks

The Surrey Commercial group of docks lie on the south side of the Thames about 3.5 km below London Bridge. The actual layout was the result of a gradual development by numerous operators, commencing with the Howland Great Wet Dock at the end of the 17th century and culminating in the amalgamation of the two surviving companies under the name of the Surrey Commercial Dock Company in 1864.

The majority of the docks then consisted of ponds and open sheds for the timber trade, and facilities for sea-going vessels were limited. Further construction led to the opening of the Canada Dock in 1876 and to the completion of the Greenland Dock and the Canada-Greenland Passage during the period 1898 - 1904. Built on the site of Howland Great Wet Dock, the Greenland Dock was 686m long by 137m wide. Although difficulties were encountered with this work due to foundation problems and the death of the engineer, J A Maconnidue, construction was finally completed under the direction of Sir John Wolfe Barry. The entrance lock enabled the Surrey Dock

37   *The Surrey Docks on the south side of the Thames. (a) The Commercial Docks at Rotherhithe 1813 looking west from the river, from an aquatint by William Danniel. The picture includes ships on the Surrey canal. (PLA) (b) An aerial photograph of the Surrey Docks as they were before their closure in 1969. In the foreground are ships unloading timber in the Canada Dock. (LDDC)*

VIEW OF THE GRAND SURREY DOCKS CANAL

ENTRANCE TO SURREY CANAL FROM THAMES

ENTRANCE TO THE COMMERCIAL DOCKS—ROTHERHITHE

38   The Grand Surrey Canal Docks with the entrance basin and lock built at Rotherhithe in 1807. Peaceful scenes from unpublished water colours by G. Yates 1826. (PLA)

to compete directly with the West India Dock and Millwall Dock. Ships of 12,000 tonnes gross, and mainly carrying grain from Canada were accommodated by the Greenland Dock.

With the establishment of the Port of London Authority, shipping and trade requirements in the Port of London was considered as a whole, and because of the absence of railway facilities in this group of docks, limited developments were planned. In 1926, the Quebec Dock with four deep water berths was completed and three years later an impounding station was provided to maintain dock water level. Further developments took place after the Second World War.

The whole of the Surrey Docks closed in 1969 and little remains except at the southern end, although the entrance lock of Greenland Dock with its hydraulic capstans and machinery is still essentially intact. There is a public right of way over the swing footbridge crossing the lock.

Tilbury Docks

The Tilbury Docks were constructed by the East and West India Docks Company in 1886, to the designs of their engineers Mr A Manning and Mr D S Baynes. They consisted of a tidal basin having a depth of nearly 14m below Trinity High Water, communicating with the four docks by means of a lock, which was 214m long by 24m wide. The lock was provided with three pairs of iron double-skinned gates. The docks consisted of a main dock 183m wide and 545m long, with three branch docks leading off to the north side, two of which had a width of 76m and the third and centre one 92m, the length of all three being 490m. The total length of the quays in the docks and tidal basin was 3.2 km.

In addition two dry docks were provided with ship-type tank floating caissons which, by means of intermediate caissons, were divisible into shorter lengths in order to accommodate vessels of various lengths and to economise on pumping. The quays were equipped with hydraulic portal cranes and were served entirely by railways.

In 1910 Mr Frederick Palmer, then Chief Engineer of the Port Authority, formulated a series of schemes for the extension of the port and for modernising the existing docks. The extension included a westward addition in the form of a new branch dock,

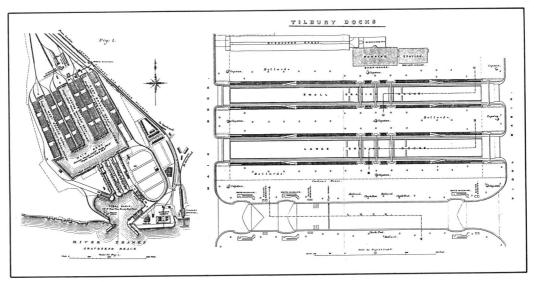

39   Map of Tilbury Docks constructed by the East and West India Docks Company in 1886 to the design of their Engineers A Manning and D S Baynes. They are the only surviving old docks of the Port of London Authority which are still in use. (ICE)

a new entrance and two dry docks. They were constructed by Jones and Railton Ltd in August 1916. A new entrance lock was constructed in 1928 together with a quay at the inner end on the north side. In 1957 a long return quay was constructed and the Main Dock was widened from 183m to 275m enabling ships up to 214m long to turn into the then existing West Branch Dock.

From the mid 1960s considerable investment was made in new facilities at Tilbury to cater for the new, large and specialised vessels coming into service and the plant required to handle the varied forms of cargoes. Because the new vessels required deep water, a £30m dock extension was constructed at Tilbury with a deep water quay providing 13 new berths - including six container ship berths. With these changes came the building of

the Rail Container Terminal with the dock area connecting to the national rail network.

A huge bulk grain terminal was also constructed at Tilbury capable of holding 100,000 tonnes and taking vessels up to 83,000 tonnes. Next to it, four privately owned flour mills fed from the terminal were also built.

As part of the development work, a riverside roll-on roll-off facility was added to the existing Passenger Landing Stage in 1973. This was followed in 1974 by a multi-million pound purpose built general cargo/unitised cargo/package timber/ container terminal, initially to handle the West African trade. In 1978, the new £24m Northfleet Hope deep water riverside container terminal became operational.

The Thames Barrier, opened in May 1984, was the last major construction project, at a cost of 450 million pounds, in the Port of London. The firm of consulting engineers was Rendel, Palmer & Tritton, founded by Sir Frederick Palmer previously the Chief Engineer of the Port of London Authority.

The barrier, the world's largest moveable flood gates, straddles the river Thames at Woolwich south of the Royal Docks. It consists of a set of piers between which are huge steel sector gates. During a flood alert, the gates are raised hydraulically to prevent the incoming high surge tides rushing upstream and hence stop devastation to more than a third of the capital. (NCE)

Surviving Engineering and Architectural Features

Historic Buildings

Sadly during the last decade much evidence of the port's history has disappeared and what remains is at risk. Buildings and warehouses have been demolished, machinery removed for scrap and company records, photographs, drawings and other documents destroyed and dispersed. The memories of men and women who spent their lives working in the docks still remain unrecorded. It is hoped that in future much more recording and renovation work on buildings will be undertaken.

This section includes a brief survey of some of the surviving engineering and architectural features in the docklands starting from the western boundary at Tower Bridge. This bridge is one of the most famous bridges in the world, built during 1886-94 in Gothic style to blend with the nearby historic buildings of the Tower of London. The stonework conceals a semi-suspended steel framework and has no structural function. The engineer for the work was Sir John Wolfe Barry and the architect was Sir Horace Jones. The bridge bascules were raised by hydraulic power, the engines being housed in the bases of the piers, while power was supplied from a pumping station on the south side. Hydraulic Lifts in the towers give access to the overhead walkway which is now open to the public as a tourist attraction.

In the St. Katharine Docks, the Eastern Dock, Western Dock and the entrance basin of the original construction have survived. In 1969 the Port of London Authority sold the docks to the Greater London Council for £1.5m which was £500,000 less than the original cost in 1828. Seven developers put forward schemes and the contractors, Taylor Woodrow were granted a 125 year lease on the site. They built the Tower Hotel in 1973 and turned the dock into a marina. A collection of historic ships is housed in the Eastern Dock.

The redevelopment of the London Docks are now complete. The major surviving building is the "Skin Floor" which is a substantial part of the New Tobacco Warehouse. It has the best preserved brick groin vaults in Docklands.

Designed and built by Daniel Alexander, Surveyor to the London Dock Company, between 1811-1813, the 2 ha warehouse was used for the storage of tobacco and wine. The building with a floor area of 20,000 square metres, was later

40   *Tower Bridge at the western boundary of London Docklands is one of the most famous bridges in the world, completed in 1894 in Gothic style to blend with the nearby Tower of London. The design Engineer was Sir John Wolfe-Barry and the Architect was Sir Horace Jones. The bridge has recently been floodlit to become the "Gateway to London" by night, June 1988. (NCE)*

41   *The famous Tobacco Warehouses (The "Skin Floor") built in 1813 for the London Dock Company, remains the best preserved and largest extent of brick groin vaults in Docklands. (a) An external view from the south side. (b) The interior of the warehouses in July 1970. The buildings were constructed over the vaults as a series of large span timber queen-post roof trusses, supported by bifurcated cast iron columns with a tree-like form and surrounded by brick enclosing walls. The structural use of cast iron is one of the oldest in the world. (GLRO)*

25

42   Butler's Wharf formed the largest group of warehouses completed in 1873 on either side of Shad Thames, Bermondsey SE1. The architect was James Tolley and the contractor John Aird & Son. (a) This photograph shows Wharf No 15 1981. (GLRO) (b) The derelict warehouses 1984. (LDDC)

43   The Free Trade Wharf, The Highway, Wapping E1. The 19th century warehouses surround the historic saltpetre store of the East India Dock Company which dates from 1795. The warehouses are being developed into luxury homes. (a) The derelict warehouses 1981. (GLRO) (b) The converted warehouses of luxury homes 1988. (Reglian Group)

44   Gun Wharves near Wapping Station are Grade 2 listed. The former tea and spice warehouses lining both sides of Wapping High Street have been converted into luxury homes. (a) The riverside wharves with cranes 1981. (GLRO) (b) The restored buildings 1987. (LDDC)

used for the storage of valuable imported furs and was therefore named as the "Skin Floor". It was constructed over the vaults as a single-storeyed structure with timber queen-post roof trusses of 16.5m span. The trusses were supported by bifuracted cast iron columns with a tree-like form with raking struts supporting alternate roof trusses midway between the columns. Recently, a scheme has been prepared for the restoration of the four bays of the Skin Floor warehouse with the vaults beneath and the construction of a two-level car park.

South of the river, Butler's Wharf forms the largest number of warehouses and wharves on the Thames, 17 of which are listed buildings. They were completed in 1873 on either side of Shad Thames in Bermondsey. The architects were Tolley and Dale and the builder John Aird & Son. The buildings were owned by Butler's Wharf Ltd, which became public in 1872, its origins going back to the late 18th century when a Mr Butler was associated with the company. Developers Conran Roche are

shed and was raised to its present height in 1827 by Sir John Rennie, son of John Rennie, to cope with the trade expansion of the West India Dock Company from the Far East. The warehouse was destroyed by fire in 1901 but the timber structure was restored.

To the west side of the warehouses, the quadrangle building, now known as Cannon Workshops, was built in 1824 for the West India Dock Company by Sir John Rennie, to provide offices, engineering workshops, stores and cooperage. An original forge from 1825 still remains. Outside the engineers' office is a cast-iron plaque 'THW 1800' indicating Trinity High Water level, the datum level of the Port of London.

The House Mill rebuilt in 1776 and the Clock Mill rebuilt in 1817 are the only surving tidal mills in the Dockland and are the largest in the country. The buildings are on a site near Stratford in Newham which has been used as a distillery since

45   The Georgian Dockmaster House on the Isle of Dogs was designed in 1807 by Thomas Morris, the Engineer to the West India Dock Company and it has had a number of uses. This photograph shows the building after its renovation in 1986. (LDDC)

46   The Ledger Building at the entrance to the West India Docks was designed by the Architect George Guilt in 1808. It has been renovated and used by the London Dockland Development Corporation as administrative offices. 1987 (LDDC)

restoring and regenerating the 5.6 ha site to provide homes, shops, studios and riverside activities.

St Saviour's Dock on the Surrey side has several surviving mills and warehouses mainly from 1850-1900 which are Grade 2 listed as part of Southwark Conservation Area. St George's Wharf has small cast iron windows and bands of blue bricks. Lime Wharf is a red brick building with a gabled sack hoist. New Concordia Wharf was part of St Saviour's flour mill rebuilt 1894-98 after a fire. The mill has a fine brick chimney. These warehouses have been converted into luxury flats.

At the entrance to the West India Docks on the Isle of Dogs, stands the Georgian Dockmaster's House designed in 1807 by Thomas Morris, the engineer to the West India Dock Company. It was first used as an excise office, then became the Jamaica Tavern, reverting under the PLA to Dock Manager's office. It was empty until 1987, when it was sold.

Nearby, stands the last surviving group of multi-storey ware-houses from the early period of dock construction. Warehouses 1 and 2 were designed by the architect George Guilt, and were later modified by the engineer John Rennie. Warehouse 2, opened in 1802, had originally a timber frame interior but cast-iron stanchions were inserted by John Rennie in 1841 due to overloading. Sugar, which arrived in hogsheads, was the main product stored here. Warehouse 1 was originally a low

1927. There are four 500 mm diameter undershot wheels in the House Mill and three in the Clock Mill. The Passmore Edwards Museum is restoring the first building as a museum of Social History while the second building has been converted into offices.

The impressive Abbey Mills Pumping Station in Newham was designed in Gothic style by the engineer Sir Joseph Bazalgette and the architect Vulliamy for the Metropolitan Board of Works and construction was completed in 1868. The station is now used for pumping sewage from the London Boroughs to Becton and Abbey Creek. The old beam engines were replaced in 1972 by electrically driven and diesel driven engines.

There are a large number of buildings, sheds and warehouses existing in the Royal Docks. The former Gallions Hotel designed by the architects Vigers and Wagstaffe was built in 1883 on the north quay of Albert Basin for the use of liner passengers. The hotel was constructed on piles and had stables below the ground floor. The same architect designed the Connaught Tavern in 1881 at Connaught Road, which is a large public house in Queen Anne style.

Warehouses K and W on the north quay of the Royal Victoria Dock are Grade 2 listed buildings. Both built in 1883, the construction was of timber floors on cast-iron columns with

47   Warehouses 1 and 2 on the Isle of Dogs are the last surviving group of historic buildings on the North Quay of the Import Dock in the West India Dock. They formed part of nine warehouses designed by George Guilt as the Architect and William Jessop as the Engineer in 1800. The other seven warehouses were destroyed during the bombing of 1940. (a) The empty warehouses 1985. (b) A north view of the same in 1972. (LDDC) (c) A view of the original warehouses from an aquatint by Bluck after a picture by Rowlandson and Pugin 1810. (PLA)

external brick walls under a slate roof while the ground floor was of concrete. The upper floors were used for the storage of tobacco. Since 1983 the W warehouse has been used as an exhibition centre by the Museum in Dockland. The other remaining sheds and buildings were constructed mainly in the period 1920 to 1963.

Dock Structures and Cranes

The Royal Docks, which were closed in 1985 but are still intact, contain many examples of dock structures. Three dry docks exist, two of these being accessible from the Royal Albert Dock while the other one is situated at the western end of King George V Dock. The latter is approximately 230m long by 30m wide. The associated pumping station has fallen into disuse and has been allowed to flood, immersing the existing pumping equipment.

Originally there were four lock entrances to the docks. At the present time, only one is unfilled, this being the entrance to King George V Dock. The lock is hydraulically powered by the PLA's own equipment which has since replaced that of the London Hydraulic Company. Midway along this lock is situated a large moveable steel structure which is part of London's flood defences and is designed to block the lock entrance at the same time as the Thames Flood Barrier is operated. To supplement this the PLA have a large floating caisson in King George V Dock.

There are approximately 40 types of dock walls, many of which form the Royal Victoria Dock. In this dock most of these walls are of sheet piled construction, with or without concrete jetties in front of them, tied back to piles or existing foundations, thus in many instances demolition of buildings has to be assessed in conjunction with wall stability. In the late 1930s, a major modification of the deep water quay along the north side of the dock was undertaken which consisted of a suspended reinforced concrete deck supported by a system of precast piles. The general construction of the walls for the Royal Albert Dock was a mass concrete retaining wall of stepped type counterfronted at intervals.

The condition of some timber jetties is poor and should not be utilised in future redevelopment without careful consideration. The two long quays on the north side of the Royal Victoria and Royal Albert Docks were built to provide deepwater berths. They are constructed of reinforced concrete and project out over the water from the north quay of both docks. Beneath these suspended quays the dock shallows and large quantities of silt exist. Most of the cranes in good working condition have been transferred by the PLA for use in the Tilbury Docks. There are about 54 quayside cranes on tracks of which 48 are in the Albert and King George V Docks and 6 in the Victoria Dock area. The majority of these cranes are of 5 tons lifting capacity at 24.0m radius and were manufactured by Stothert & Pitt of Bath during 1963-64, although there are some which appeared to be older. The cranes are electrically operated and appear to be in satisfactory structural condition, although there is rusting due to lack of maintenance.

At the west end of the Victoria Dock and adjacent to Shed G, a fixed derrick crane of 11.25 tonnes capacity is located. The crane was manufactured by John Henderson of Aberdeen, is electrically driven and is supported on three concrete piers. Since it was last used in 1983 there has been considerable deterioration.

48   Abbey Mills Pumping Station in Newham. (a) The Victorian A Station 1968. (b) The interior of A Station 1955. (GLRO)

Dockland Museums

In St. Katharine Docks, there is a display of Maritime Trust ships including, in the East Basin, Captain Scott's Discovery (1901) with her new yards and rigging. The steam herring drifter Lydia Eve, Robin and other vessels can also be seen in the same docks. Shipyards in Dockland built most 18th century Royal Navy vessels including the Great Eastern, the largest ship of the last century. The John Mackay, probably the oldest steam-driven ship in the world, is berthed at Canary Wharf and other historic vessels are being offered facilities to attract tourists. The National Maritime Museum is seeking to establish a Boat Museum on the Isle of Dogs.

With the aid of a grant from the London Docklands Development Corporation, the Passmore Edwards Museum of Newham converted the North Woolwich old Railway Station into a museum. The station building was built for the opening of the Eastern Counties Railway extension to North Woolwich on 14th June 1847. The Museum contains many objects and features which illustrate the history of the Great Eastern Railway, including a restored ticket office of the period 1914 to 1939. Track lines have been relaid and there is a live operation of steam engines.

David Kirkaldy, a Scottish Engineer from the Clydeside shipbuilding industry, established the first materials testing laboratory at The Grove, Southwark, in 1864. The success of this pioneer venture led to the building in 1873 of purpose-built accommodation, designed by T R Smith, at 99 Southwark Street. This building, currently housing Kirkaldy's unique patent hydraulic testing machine of 1864, has been set up as a materials testing museum which is open to the public on occasions.

In 1982, the Museum of London proposed the setting up of the Museum in Docklands and soon afterwards a major dedicated operation was conducted to rescue and collect objects relating to life and work in East London. In October 1986 The Museum opened its Visitor Centre in W Warehouse in the Royal Victoria Dock for a preview of the Museum's exhibits. The collection included many items ranging from dock hooks to carts, winches, cranes, boats and tugs. Dockland trades represented included cooperage, rigger's workshop, cargo handling, tobacco weighing, shipbuilding and printers' work-shop. It is anticipated that the first phase of the Museum in Docklands featuring floating, quayside and indoor exhibits, will open at the North Quay of the West India Dock in the near future.

50   A mechanized scene at the Albert Dock in the late 1960s with car components being exported to New Zealand. The majority of the cranes used were 5 tonnes lifting capacity at 24 m radius manufactured by Stothbert & Pitt of Bath. (PLA)

51   North Woolwich Railway Station, opened on 14 June 1847, has recently been converted into a museum, featuring the history of the Great Eastern Railway. (LDDC)

49   Surviving buildings in the Royal Dock. (a) Warehouse W on the north quay of the Royal Victoria Dock photographed January 1917. The upper floors were used for the storage of tobacco. (b) Front elevation of K to S Warehouses 1977. (LDDC)

Present Use and Steps Towards Redevelopment

Port of London

The Port of London still stretches about 150 km up the Thames to the river's tidal limit at Teddington weir and within this area there exists a variety of facilities and wharves for handling cargo of all types. The Port of London Authority (PLA) owns and operates only the docks at Tilbury for the handling of containers, roll-on roll-off traffic and bulk cargoes. The private riverside wharves and facilities are scattered from Gravesend to Brentford and handle a substantial cargo up the river. Other major traffic along the Thames belongs to installations of oil, gas and manufacturing companies.

Tilbury Docks have the most comprehensive range of modern cargo handling facilities in the UK. Every type of cargo handling operation is performed within the docks. Each year the terminal, wharves and berths handle 45 million tonnes of cargo, 7 million of which are related to existing facilities in London Docklands. The PLA is responsible for the licensing of private wharves, watermen and lightermen, dredging and salvage and the provision of navigational and communication services. These services are funded by charges raised on vessels and goods coming into the Thames. The PLA has a POLARIS computer based navigational system for the Thames, which monitors 13,000 intra-port movements each year.

Over 60 shipping companies operate various types of services from London to 100 ports all over the world. Towage on the Thames is performed by 15 tugs of the Alexandra Towing Co Ltd, 9 of which having full fire-fighting facilities while the PLA has its own tugs within Tilbury Docks. Nearly 100 passenger ships call at Tilbury each year and amenities have been improved at the London Cruise Terminal in recognition of the growing needs of this traffic.

Docklands Redevelopment

Discussions on the future of Docklands have been going on for the past 15 years. In January 1973 a study by Messrs. R Travers Morgan (Consulting Engineers) sponsored jointly by the Department of the Environment and the Greater London Council, produced various schemes for the redevelopment which were the basis of public debate but none of these schemes found much favour and they were largely shelved as a result. In 1974 the GLC and the Dockland boroughs joined forces to establish the Docklands Joint Committee with major responsibility for preparing an overall plan - a strategy to co-ordinate planning and development within the area. In July 1976, this committee published the Docklands strategic plan which marked a major step towards redevelopment of the area, based on months of public debate and searching analysis.

The overall objective of the strategy was "To use the opportunity provided by large areas of London's Docklands becoming available for development to redress the housing, social environmental, industrial, economic and communications deficiencies of the Docklands and parent boroughs and thereby to provide the freedom for similar improvements through east and inner London".

Despite considerable effort, new industry did not take the place of the old and 8,500 jobs were lost between 1975 and 1980. Thus a shrinking population found itself isolated among wide tracts of derelict land and buildings.

In 1981 the London Docklands Development Corporation (LDDC) was created and charged with the regeneration of the area. The corporation is a statutory body appointed and funded by central government. A comprehensive programme of land acquisition, housing and infrastructure provision has transformed Docklands into a major growth area in London. Numerous companies have moved into the area since the formation of the corporation and private investment commitments have been considerable in some of the most ambitious development in the world. Projects already completed include Billingsgate Fish Market, Cannon Workshops, Teltscher Brothers Wine Complex and various business parks.

Docklands Light Railway

Two new transport schemes have been constructed which are essential for the current regeneration and future development of the London Docklands. In a joint venture with General Electric Company (GEC). John Mowlem plc has built the Docklands Light Railway at a cost of £77m for the London Regional Transport. Atkins Partners have supplied a multidisciplinary consultancy service for the project. The 12km railway, the first of its kind in Britain, opened in July 1987, linking the Isle of Dogs with Stratford and the City. It uses Light Rail Technology which means automated trains of light construction operating on a combination of existing railway tracks and new tracks. Practically the whole of the railway is elevated, either on the old brick Limehouse viaduct or new purpose built structure. The railway is the first new route in London since 1940 and it extends in an area which has not seen trains since the closing of the old London & Blackwall railway in the 1920s.

Plans have been approved for an extension westwards to the heart of the City at the Bank. Plans are also in hand for increasing the capacity of the railway to serve the proposed new development at Canary Wharf on the Isle of Dogs and for extension of the track eastwards to the Royal Docks and Beckton.

52   *Tilbury Docks are the only surviving old docks operated by the Port of London Authority. (a) A view of the docks when opened April 1886. (ILN) (b) An aerial photograph of the docks 100 years later in 1986. (PLA)*

London City Airport

Contractors, John Mowlem ppc have also been working closely with the Port of London Authority (PLA) in the development and construction of Britain's first short take-off and landing airport at a cost of around £30m. The Stolport, recently given the name of London City Airport, was opened in October 1987 and is only a short car journey to the centre of London. The airstrip, being 762m long and built on a 36ha site between the Royal Albert and King George V Docks, is considered a major project in the redevelopment of the Royal Docks in Newham.

It is designed to handle up to 1.2 million passengers a year using 50 seater four engined turbo-prop aircraft developed specifically for operating in urban areas and restricted sites. Airline operators have already services to provide links with UK and European airports within the 650km range of Stol aircraft. Destinations include Paris, Brussels, Antwerp, Amsterdam, Rotterdam, Frankfurt and Dusseldorf, plus the domestic airports at Glasgow, Belfast, Manchester and the Channel Islands.

The airport terminal building will have all the facilities associated with a main airport including viewing areas, shops, offices, cafes and a restaurant overlooking the King George V Dock.

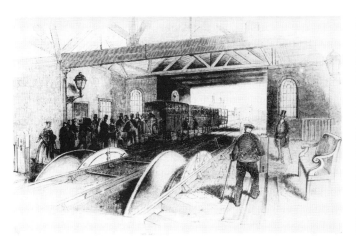

53   The old Blackwall Railway. Chains were used to draw the original London-Poplar Rail in the nineteenth century. (LDDC)

55   Brick viaducts built in 1872 to carry the cable hauled railway were refurbished in 1986 to carry the Docklands Light Railway across Millwall Park on the Isle of Dogs. (LDDC)

54   Dockland Light Railway opened July 1987, the first of the type in Britain. (a) A train seen at Shadwell Station bound for the Isle of Dogs. (LDDC). (b) An automatic train crossing the new elevated bridge over the former West India Docks.

56   *London City Airport (Stolport) in the Royal Docks was opened 1987, as Britain's first short take-off airport. Conceived in 1981 by John Mowlem & Co., the airport links with UK and European airports. (a) An aerial view of the airport and runway south of Albert Dock. (LDDC) (b) General view of the Royal Docks showing the location of the airport April 1988. (Handford)*

Current and Future Development In Docklands

London Docklands are now recognized as the largest and most successful urban redevelopment and renewal in the world and the biggest that has been undertaken in London since the Great Fire in 1666. Utilizing the dock water areas as unique environmental and development features, numerous commercial, industrial and residential projects have been developed.

Docklands have the largest concentration of construction projects in the UK. Major infrastructure works, including roads and services are being installed to cater for the large number of new schemes, including housing estates, office blocks, light industries, sporting and other amenities. House prices have increased as purchasers compete to buy homes and flats ranging from £500,000 penthouses in converted historic warehouses to small town houses at starting prices of over £70,000. Regeneration is fastest on the Isle of Dogs and the western part of the Docklands which is nearest to the city centre. Recently land prices have sharply risen from £15,000/ha to £3.0m/ha.

There are four main development areas within Docklands: Wapping, Isle of Dogs, Surrey Docks and the Royal Docks. The present population of Docklands is around 40,000 and this is expected to double during the next few years. Encouraging investment in the future of the London Docklands was the creation of the Enterprise Zone in 1982 on the Isle of Dogs. Exemption from local rates on commercial and industrial companies moving into the zone will run until 1992. Various tax incentives are a further encouragement to businesses.

Overseas investors and organisations have taken considerable interest in Docklands' development. The Canadians are proposing to spend £3 billion on the Canary Wharf project on the Isle of Dogs, The Danes have built a housing estate in Surrey Dock. Dutchmen have developed a riverside housing area known as the London Yard. Similar ventures are planned by funds from the Swedes, Australians, Africans, Germans, Italians, Indians and elsewhere. China is planning a new Chinatown to boost her trade with Europe.

Wapping

Wapping is located within easy reach of the City of London. News International, the newspaper publishers, have built their new printing works just off the Highway. Taylor Woodrow's World Trade Centre, on the north-west corner of St Katharine Dock, provides a focal base for international companies. On the south-west corner of the site, once occupied by tea warehouses, the large Tower Hotel has been built overlooking the dock. Ivory House built in 1854 as the centre of London Ivory trade, has been converted into prestigious apartments in the upper floors and the quay level has been enclosed for shops and a yacht club. There are developments in the Free Trade Wharf and Limehouse Basin, while industrial and commercial sites are available at Thomas More Street and Wapping Lane.

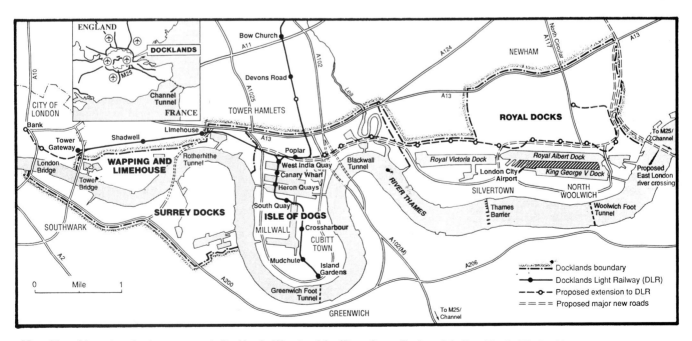

57   Map of the main redevelopment areas in Docklands: Wapping, Isle of Dogs, Surrey Docks and the Royal Docks. The Docklands Light Railway connects the area to the City of London 1988. (LDDC)

Gun Place and Gun Wharves near Wapping Station are Grade 2 listed former tea and spice warehouses lining both sides of Wapping High Street. The riverside buildings, five to seven storeys high, were built late 19th century/early 20th century. They have just been converted by house builders, Barrett East London, into luxury flats and penthouses.

One of the impressive conversions undertaken at Wapping was at Pier Head, where two attractive three-storey terraces of houses built in 1811-13 for the officers of the London Dock Company were refurbished. Nearby Oliver's Wharf was the first warehouse conversion into flats in the Docklands in 1970. The typical red brick Victorian riverside warehouses along Wapping High Street, which constituted the St John's Wharf, were beautifully refurbished in 1978.

Regalian Homes are currently working on the developing of Free Trade Wharf which is situated between the Shadwell and Limehouse Basins. The Wharf consists of a group of 19th Century warehouses surrounding a historic building which was erected in 1795 by the East India Company for storing saltpetre. The £100m conversion of the Wharf buildings includes a mixed residential and commercial complex around a central piazza, all overlooking the basins.

The London Hydraulic Power Company built their Pumping Station in 1892 at Wapping Wall. Coal was delivered to the adjacent Shadwell Basin from which water was also obtained for the station. It was modernised in the 1950s by the installation of replacement electric pumps but was finally

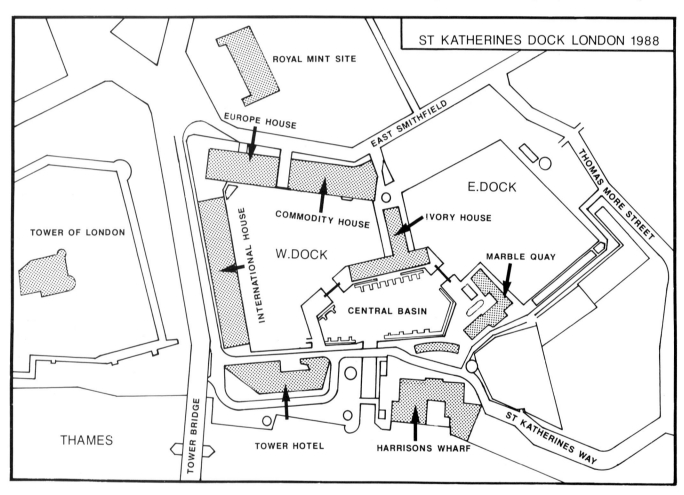

58   Map of restoration and regeneration in St Katharine Docks 1988. (St Katharine by the Tower)

The Grade 1 listed New Tobacco Warehouse at Tobacco Dock was built during 1811-13 by the London Dock company at Wapping. The warehouse was used to store tobacco and wine until the 1860s when it was converted to a wool and fur store until the 1960s and then switched to storing wine and spirits. It is imaginatively being converted into a shopping complex twice the size of Covent Garden. The impressive brick vaults are also to be refurbished and converted to shops. The ground floor is being modified to provide a huge shopping precinct under the original timber trussed roof.

The site of Western Dock, once busy with stevedores unloading kegs of brandy, tobacco and other luxury goods, is being developed into 1000 houses and flats around small squares, landscaped courts and public walkways.

closed in 1977. Plans are in hand to convert the station into a modern recording studio for the Academy of St Martin-in-the-Fields. The new home will have observation platforms for the public to watch the orchestra's rehearsals. The development will mean an expansion of the social life in the area.

Limehouse, which lies between Wapping and the entrance to the Isle of Dogs, has recently attracted many well known personalities. The oldest part of the area is Narrow Street in which some of the houses date back to the early eighteenth century. At the western end of this street, some warehouses are being converted into individually designed units with open plan accommodation looking southwards along the Thames.

59   The old St Katharine Docks as they were in 1968 viewed from the south. The beautiful B warehouses are on the left of the picture. Ivory House is on the central Island. The empty area on the right is the site of the other warehouses demolished following the bombing of the Second World War in the 1940s. Note the adjacent warehouses and jetty of the London Docks. (St Katharine by the Tower)

60   St Katharine Docks today, a superb example of urban regeneration. An aerial view from the north in March 1987 shows Ivory House (1854), Commodity Quay (1987), World Trade Centre (1982) and the Tower Hotel (1973) with Tower Bridge in the background (St Katharine by the Tower)

61   Ivory House in St Katharine Docks. (a) The warehouse built in 1854 as the centre of the London Ivory Trade, has been restored to provide prestigious apartments on the upper floors and shops and a yacht club at the quay level.
(b) Wine vaults under Ivory House have been restored to form a beautiful barrel - vaulted ceiling banqueting Hall 1988. (St Katharine by the Tower)

62   Oliver's Wharf and Wapping Pierhead were the first warehouse converted into flats in Docklands in the 1970s. (a) A view of the Victorian Gothic warehouse with two lighters along the river 1971. (GLRO) (b) The restored buildings 1981. (LDDC)

64   An aerial photograph of the Tobacco Warehouses and redevelopment of the London Docks at Wapping. The filling and redevelopment of the Docks are now practically complete 1988. (Handford).

63   London, the River and the Docks on 30 August 1968. A bird's eye view of the city showing Shadwell Basin, Eastern and Western Basins of London Docks and St Katharine Docks shortly before their closures. (Handford)

65   The Grade I listed Tobacco Warehouse (The "Skin Floor") was built in Wapping during 1811-13 by the London Dock Company. It is being imaginatively converted into a shopping complex twice the size of Covent Garden 1988. (a) A perspective of the exterior of the development. (b) A cross-section of the interior of the shopping city. (Tobacco Dock Developments)

66   *The Tobacco Warehouse in the old days. (a) A view of the interior January 1857. The premises stored casks of tabacco brought into the Port of London. Note the pair of scales and the pulley arrangements. (ILN) (b) A view of the impressive brick wine vaults, prior to refurbishment 1987. (Tobacco Dock Developments)*

67   *Shadwell Basin regeneration at Wapping 1988. Major housing development has been undertaken around the Basin and in the filled Eastern Basin of the old London Docks. The historic warehouses of Metropolitan Wharf (shown in the picture with a temporary access bridge from the river) are also being converted into magnificent apartments overlooking the Thames. (Handford)*

Isle of Dogs

In the Isle of Dogs, developments are taking place over the whole area with over 200 companies having moved into new buildings. Printers, publishers, television companies, and computer firms are some of the business developments which also include the Daily Telegraph, the Guardian, Northern and Shell and Limehouse Studios and the construction of the first Mercury satellite station. Many new offices and industrial units have been built by John Laing, Wimpeys, Waites, Costain and Indescon. Asda have opened a new superstore next to the Enterprise Zone.

The initial stage of development was confined to small-scale and low-rise buildings for light industry and general business. Examples of these units exist around Cannon Workshop. Skylines at the top of East Ferry Road was completed by John Laing Developments Ltd early in 1986. This is an enclosed business park of 36 attractive self-contained office buildings of medium size.

Since the announcement in 1985 by the Bank of England that financial services organisations could be located outside the traditional inner city areas, Docklands have been earmarked as the new financial centre of the world. Already many schemes are planned. The proposed international finance centre at

Canary Wharf in the West India Docks, where once tomatoes from the Canary Islands were imported, will cost over £3,000m and will break the UK national records for its size. This project, originally proposed by a consortium of American and Swiss Banks, will create the most comprehensive and coherent dynamic business community in Europe. Architects, engineers and planners are working on the technical approvals and construction documentation for this massive scheme. It occupies a site of 29ha and is designed to provide buildings totalling more than one million square metres of office accommodation. Two thirds of the space will be landscaped open space with a public piazza twice the size of Trafalgar Square.

The Canadian developers, Olympia and York bought the interest in the summer of 1987 and started their piling work for the scheme in March 1988. They have adopted the plans envisaged by the American originator, G Ware Travel Ltd., whose group withdrew due to lack of cash.

The Canary Wharf Development Company will develop 22 major buildings with retail and leisure facilities. There will be two 400-bed hotels, 6500 car parking spaces and a series of interconnected landscaped courtyards, parks and plazas. Canary Wharf will be built in two phases over the next seven to ten years.

Situated in London Enterprise Zone, Heron Quays on the West India Docks is one of the first waterside developments to be completed by Tarmac Brook Glade Properties. The Swedish-style blocks provide prestigious offices, business apartments and amenity buildings. Courtyards and squares have been created to give a Venice-like setting for a working and living environment.

Another redevelopment project has begun at Harbour Exchange. The development provides for a range of self-contained buildings with leisure facilities including retail shops, walkways, a central piazza, business apartments and conference facilities. The site is bounded by West India House on the southern side and Dockland Light Railway viaduct on the northern boundary, allowing the complete western elevation to front along the quayside. Like other schemes in the enterprise zone, there are no rates to pay until 1992 and a 100% first year corporate tax allowance against full development cost.

Trafalgar House Group, jointly with other developers, have plans to convert the Ledger Buildings and the adjacent Warehouses 1 and 2 of the Import Dock into shopping and entertainment facilities. The multi-storey warehouses at the northern end of the West India Docks were constructed during 1802-6 by Napoleonic prisoners of war to the designs of the engineer William Jessop. When built they formed the largest warehouse complex in the world and they are now the last surviving extensive group of early dock buildings.

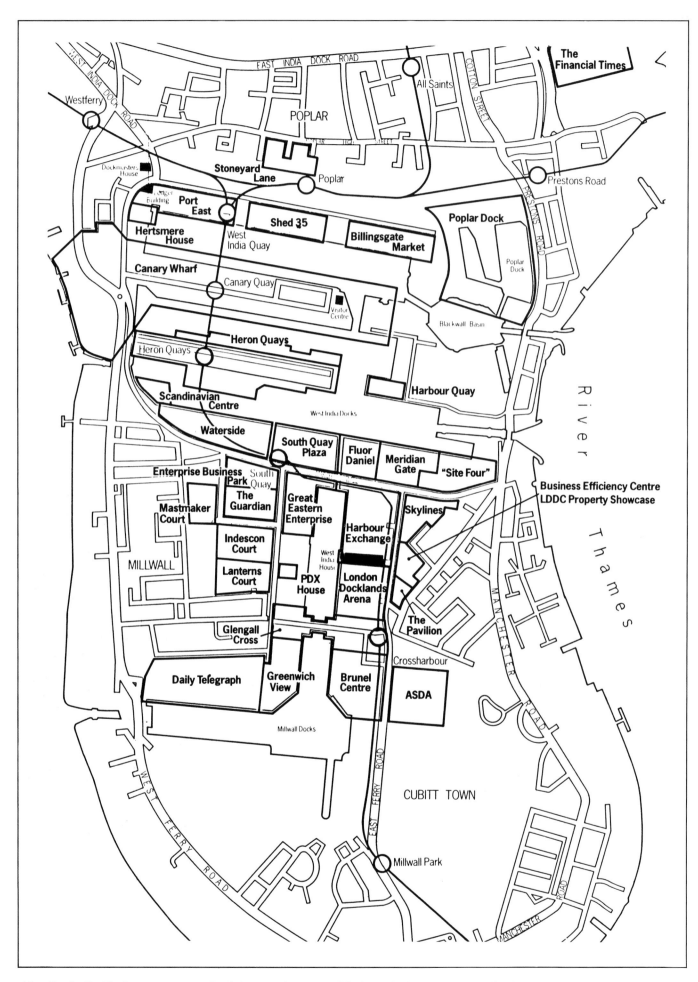

68 *London Docklands are now recognized as the largest and most successful urban redevelopment and renewal in the world and the biggest that has been undertaken in London since the Great Fire of 1666. This map shows the projects completed or proposed on the Isle of Dogs and its Enterprise Zone 1988. (LDDC).*

A new office block development by Barclays Bank is Hertsmere House on West Quay, completed in the Spring of 1988. Located along the north west wide of the Import Dock, the building will be close to the proposed Canary Wharf and Port East developments. It will provide open plan banking facilities with specialist departments and Bureau de Change.

Waterside is one of the successful schemes being developed by Wiggins Group plc in association with the Port of London Properties. The site overlooking the South Dock on the Isle of Dogs has self-contained business apartments and headquarter buildings.

South Quay Plaza Phase Two is a prestigious office block development with a covered parking space and waterside location on South Dock (adjacent to the South Quay Station of Docklands Light Railway). It will have its own shopping piazza and opened for business in summer 1988. The first phase of this development was pre-sold to the Daily Telegraph which has moved its journalists and office staff out of Fleet Street to this building.

The Green at Clippers Quay, off East Ferry Road, is a development of waterside homes with mooring rights, facing Millwall Dock. At the adjacent Graving Dock, famous clipper ships such as the Cutty Sark were brought in for maintenance and repair in the late 19th century.

London Yard is a development of 300 homes designed by Building Design Partnership for the Dutch developers VOM UK. It is situated along Manchester Road on the east side of the Isle of Dogs and within a few minutes walk of Glengall Grove station of the Docklands Light Railway.

Waites are building 500 waterside homes at James Town Harbour overlooking Blackwall Basin, the first non-tidal entrance basin for the West India Docks. It is named Virginia Moorings after the pioneer settlers who sailed from Blackwall in 1606 on the ship Godspeed to set up the first English colony in America at Jamestown Virginia. The development is a second phase of a big scheme which will transform a former trading dock into a pleasant residential area.

69   *Urban regeneration on the Isle of Dogs - Britain's biggest building site and the world's most ambitious urban renewal project. This impressive aerial photograph taken 7 January 1988 shows the extensive scale of redevelopment and the numerous schemes for office blocks, housing and light industry. The elevated Docklands Light Railway winds its way gracefully across the emerging business city in East London. (Handford)*

70   A view of the derelict West India and Millwall Docks on the Isle of Dogs as they were in 1982 prior to the commencement of redevelopment by the London
Dockland Development Corporation. Note the parked lighters in the South Dock. Of the three warehouses on Canary Wharf only Limehouse Studios remains.
(LDDC)

44

71   Docklands' Dream - the Canary Wharf international finance centre on the Isle of Dogs. The centerpiece of this £3 billion development will be a 250m high tower, Britain's tallest building. (a) An artist's impression of the project from the west. (b) A view of the south promenade and buildings from Heron Quays 1988. (Olympia & York)

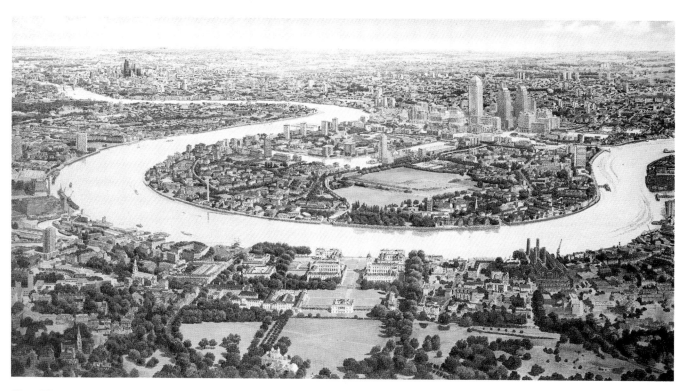

72   The future Canary Wharf Complex - The Jewel in the Docklands Crown. (a) A view of the development looking east from the River Thames. (b) A general view of the Isle of Dogs and the proposed buildings from Greenwich. (Olympia & York)

This aerial view taken in October 1989 shows how much progress has been made so far on the Canary Wharf project on the Isle of Dogs. (Olympia & York).

73   *Waterside overlooking the South Dock of the former West India Docks. It has self-contained business and residential accommodation. (LDDC)*

74   *Attractive homes in Docklands 1987. (a) The Green at Clipper's Quay, off East Ferry Road, is an estate of waterside homes with mooring rights facing Millwall Dock on the Isle of Dogs. (b) Housing development of Brunswick Quay by Daniel Homes in the Surrey Docks. (LDDC)*

75   *Surrey Docks redevelopment. Since their closure in 1969, most of these timber trade docks have been filled and many wharfside buildings demolished. (a) An aerial view looking north of the derelict docks peninsula, February 1981. (b) A photograph of the eastern area of the docks, taken January 1988, shows housing projects, the new printing and publishing works of the Daily Mail Newspaper and the Daniel Homes development overlooking the old Greenland Dock. (Handford)*

Surrey Docks

The Surrey Docks are situated south of the Thames and have a diversity of developments, the most impressive being the £450m London Bridge City with its hospital, shops, riverside walks, restaurants, 300 new homes and considerable office space. Hundreds of new houses in Surrey Quays have been created and many more are under construction. Rotherhithe and Bermondsey have their own distinctive schemes, many in historic converted warehouses. New Concordia Wharf, a renowned warehouse conversion overlooking St Saviour's Dock, has been established as one of London's luxury riverside living sites and similar developments have taken place at new Anchor Brewhouse and Butlers Wharf. Tesco Superstore are planning to build a massive shopping centre at Surrey Quays with retail units, shops and parking areas.

The Victorian warehouses of Butlers Wharf at Bermondsey are being converted into residential apartments with shops, museums and an hotel to create a 5.7 ha. riverside community

by Tower Bridge. Cinnamon Wharf, the first of the residential phase completed within Butlers Wharf, comprises 66 luxury apartments with impressive views over the waters of St Saviour's Dock or Shad Thames. The whole development is scheduled for completion by 1991.

At Butlers Wharf West, the 1895 built Boilerhouse, the Brewhouse and the Malt Mill at Shad Thames are being restored and converted into magnificent houses with excellent views over three docks. The scheme, now called the Anchor Brewhouse, offers one-bedroom units at a staggering £300,000 to £2.5 million for the spectacular four-floor Malt Mill penthouse in the original cupola and belvedere gallery.

The Vogan's Mill, a 175 year old flour grindery, is being developed into luxury flats called the New Mill Wharf at St Saviour's Dock. Vogan set up shop in 1813 in Bermondsey and moved to the present site at the end of the 19th century. Oats, lentils and barley came from various parts of the Empire to the Royal Docks, where they were then transferred into lighters and taken to Vogan's Mill. Some of the flats are due for completion late in 1989.

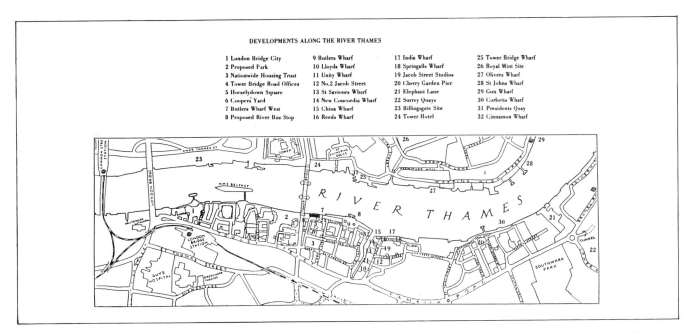

76   *Regeneration of Docklands historic warehouses. Map of commercial and residential redevelopments along the River Thames, east and west of Tower Bridge 1988. (Anchor Brewhouse Developments)*

77   London Bridge City is a most impressive commercial development revitalizing the entire South Bank, between London Bridge and Tower Bridge at the western end of Docklands, in Southwark. (a) An aerial view of the old warehouses with Hay's Dock to the left before reconstruction 1984. (b) An aerial view of the regeneration 1988. (St Martins' Property Corporation)

78   The old Hay's Dock and its fine surrounding warehouses dating from 1856. (a) A view of the east side warehouses looking north 1977. (GLRO). (b) A view of the closed dock before reconstruction began in 1986. (St Martin's Property Corporation)

79   Hay's Galleria in London Bridge City. This beautiful galleria has been completely rebuilt behind the original facade of Hay's Dock to provide shops, museums, and wine bars. (a) A view of the project from the river just before completion 1987. (LDDC) (b) The Public Square is beneath a glass barrel-vaulted roof 30m high and 90m long 1988. (c) Elevation of the development from the river 1988. (St Martin's Property Corporation)

80   New Concordia Wharf, Mill Street, Bermondsey SE1, is a renowned warehouse conversion into residential units overlooking St Saviour's Dock. (LDDC)

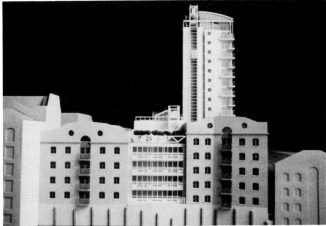

81   The Vogan's Mill in Bermondsey, SE1. The 175 years old flour grindery is being developed into luxury flats called the New Mill Wharf at St Saviour's Dock. There are two converted warehouses, a new infill block and a tower replacing the existing grain silo. (a) A view of the old Mill and warehouses 1984. (b) A model of the New Mill Wharf. (Rosebhaugh Copartnership Developments)

82   Butlers Wharf West adjacent to Tower Bridge. The 1895 built Boilerhouse, the Brewhouse and the Malt Mill at Shad Thames SE1 are being restored and converted into luxury homes now called the Anchor Brewhouse. (a) The buildings as they were before redevelopment 1984. (b) A model of the restoration by Horst Kolo. (Anchor Brewhouse Developments)

Royal Docks

The Royal Docks have the largest area of open land and water and are still largely undeveloped. Construction has started for the development of new infrastructures: roads, bridges, railways, airport, drains and sewers, etc. Over 3,000 new homes, mainly in Becton and Cyprus Place have already been built and many more are under way.

Recently three major development proposals for the Royal Dock have been prepared by the LDDC in collaboration with three private consortia. The proposals are currently under discussion with the local authority, the London Borough of Newham. A £533m development along the north side of the Royal Victoria Dock features a 25,000 seat sport stadium, a trademark and exhibition hall as well as shops, offices, an hotel and homes. A £400m proposal covers the Connaught area and the Millenium Conclear Quays on the south of the Royal Victoria Dock. It includes homes, shops, offices, studios, an hotel and a major technology centre. A £750m development along the north side of the Royal Albert Dock features a leisure, shopping and marine centre together with a science and commercial part. The basis for the disposal of the land and financing the new infrastructure for the area was approved by the Secretary of State for the Environment in March 1987.

The contents of the schemes have been under negotiation between the private developers, London Docklands Development Corporation as the development control authority, and the London Borough of Newham as the local and statutory planning authority to ensure local community needs are met. The indications are that the overall plan will go ahead subject to amendments and will form the biggest redevelopment project in Europe. This trend seems set to take the whole of the dockland development well into the 21st century.

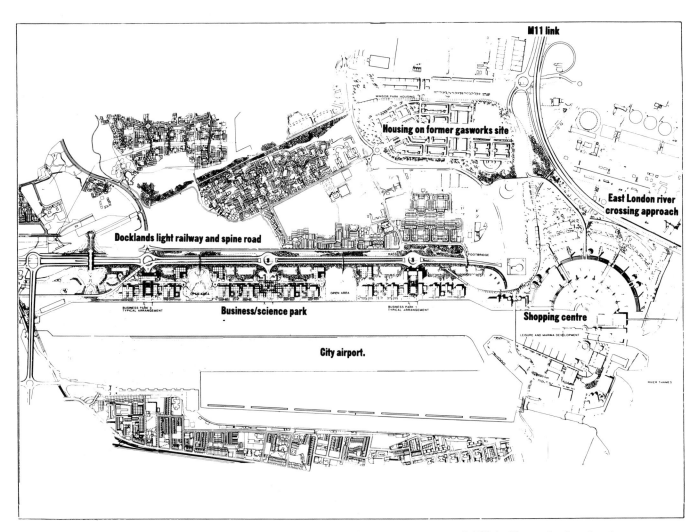

83   *Royal Albert Dock Master Plan, May 1989. The latest proposal will include a marina, a science park, 700 dwellings and a giant shopping centre. (Rosehaugh Stanhope Developments).*

84   The Royal Albert & Victoria Docks in the old days. (a) A scene looking west in the Royal Albert Dock on 13 August 1914, one day after the outbreak of the First World War. (b) The beautiful old flour mills on the south side of the Royal Victoria Dock. (PLA).

85   *The Royal Docks post 1950s. Cargoes such as frozen meat, butter, fruit, wool, grain, wine, tobacco etc., came from many corners of the world to keep London one of the greatest seaports on earth. (a) Shipping in the Royal Albert and King George V Docks on 30 August 1968. (b) The Royal Victoria Dock with the existing huge complex of reinforced concrete granaries, belonging to Rank, Spillers and CWS, which were erected during 1938–44 to replace old granaries with steam powered mills. (Hanford).*

86   The Royal Docks were the greatest port complex in the world for over a century. The 270 hectares of land and water are now ready for regeneration and form one of the largest remaining city redevelopment sites in Europe. (a) An aerial view from the west of the docks as they were after their closure in 1985. The Thames Flood Barrier is seen top right. (b) A view of the same from the east in 1988 following the opening of London City Airport on the south side of the Royal Albert Dock. (LDDC).

Short Bibliography

Further information

1   "*Dockland*", Edited by S K Al Naib with the assistance of R M J Carr, NELP/GLC, Third Printing, 1988.

2   *History of the Port of London*, Vols 1 and 2, J Broadbank, O'Connor, 1921.

3   *The Geography of the Port of London*, J Bird, Hutchinson, 1957.

4   *London's Docks*, J Pudney, Thames & Hudson, 1973.

5   *William Jessop Engineer*, C Hadfield and A W Skempton, David & Charles, 1979.

6   *London Docks*, I S Greaves, Thomas Telford, 1980.

Much relevant information will be found in magazines and reports of the Port of London Authority (PLA) and the London Docklands Development Corporation (LDDC), in Dockland News, Docklands Magazine and London Docklands Business World, and in the New Civil Engineer and Construction News, London. The NELP/GLC Dockland Book gives an illustrated historical survey of life and work in East London with an extensive list of references.

For information on present and future developments, the following organisations may be contacted:
London Docklands Development Corporation
Olympia & York Canary Wharf Ltd
St Katharine by the Tower Ltd
St Martins' Property Corporation
Tobacco Dock Developments Ltd
Anchor Brewhouse Developments Ltd
Rosehaugh Copartnership Developments
Docklands Light Railway Ltd
Heron/Mowlem/Conran Roache Consortium
Trafalgar House Residential Ltd
Laing Homes Ltd
Wiggins Property Group plc
John Mowlem Company plc
Jacobs Island Company plc
Regalian Properties plc
Kentish Property Group plc
London City Airport Ltd
Wimpey Homes Ltd
Ideal Homes Ltd
Heron Homes Ltd

Details of converted and new commercial and residential properties may be obtained from numerous estate agents operating in the area, including; Savills, Chesterton, Hamptons, Cluttons, Jones Lang Wotton, Collins Druce, Grant & Partners, Clapshaws, Healey & Baker, Alex Neil, and Carleton Smith & Co.

A regular Riverbus service is operated through London Docklands from the West India Pier to Chelsea Harbour Pier. Route information is available from Thames Line Company.

Index

References to illustrations and maps are italicised, and are numbered independently of page numbers. Maps are listed after illustrations.

Acknowledgements

I wish to thank my institution, The Polytechnic of East London (formerly North East London Polytechnic) for its support and the Commission of the European Communities (EEC) for a small grant to initiate a study on the history and development of European Ports. I am deeply indebted to many people, previous writers, and organisations for the supply of information and assistance with the research work. In particular, I am most grateful for permission to reproduce photographs and illustrations by the following:-

Port of London Authority (PLA), Dockland News and London Docklands Development Corporation (LDDC), Greater London Record Office (GLRO), Illustrated London News (ILN), BBC Hulton Picture Library (HPL), Handford Photography, Institution of Civil Engineers (ICE), New Civil Engineer (NCE), St Martins Property Corporation, The Lennard Raine Partnership, St Katharine by the Tower Ltd., Olympia & York Canary Wharf Ltd., Pollard Thomas & Edwards Architects, Tabascco Dock Developments Ltd., Conran Roache, Michael Squire Associates, Reglian Group, Anchor Brewhouse Developments Ltd., Rosehaugh Copartnership Development

I gratefully thank Terry Hutton (PLA), Carole Lyders (LDDC), Chris Denvir (GLRO), Angus Rankine (Olympia & York), Marilyn Evans (St Katharine by the Tower), Tom Samson (Hanford), Peter Lennard (The Lennard Raine Partnership) and Grant Smith (NCE).

Special thanks are due to Ted Weedon for his enthusiastic assistance and proof reading, to Walter Evans for reading the initial articles, to Simon Pattle for his kind co-operation and assistance with the preparation of photographs and illustrations, to Margaret Youngman and Carole Anthony for their excellent typing of the manuscript, to Philip Plumb for his general advice, to Barry Nottage for library assistance, to Brian Rees and Nimmi Patel of ILEA for artwork and printing, to John Noble for preparing the index, and to my wife Irene Naib for her assistance and forbearance.

I also thank many other people who helped including John Beake, Stewart Innes, Norma Jones, Derek Merrit, Derek Hart, Alan Pumfreth, Stephen Card, Ivan Greaves, Nick Carter, Kate Ellison, Desmond Bond, Elizabeth Underwood, Victor Edge, Brian Johnson, Martin O'Leary, Marc Pattinson, Mary Mills, Beverly James, Susan Hewer, Vivian Hamley and Terry Myring.

Dr S K Al Naib
Head of Department of Civil Engineering
The Polytechnic of East London
Longbridge Road
Dagenham
Essex RM8 2AS
England